MEMACE BOOK 2000

THIS BOOK BELONGS TO

Callum

sundilands

Printed and Published by D. C. THOMSON & CO., LTD., 185 Fleet Street, London, EC4A 2HS.
© D. C. THOMSON & CO., LTD., 1999
ISBN 0 85116 706 3

I ACCEPT! I CHOOSE MUD PIES FOR WEAPONS!

OOH, MAYBE THIS WASN'T SUCH A GOOD IDEA! I'LL GET DIRTY!

OR MAYBE I WON'T.

RUMBLE OF TROTTERS

THAT SOUNDS LIKE...

...RASH*ERK!*

BOOMF

YOU MIGHT BE MY MASTER, BUT NOBODY TOUCHES MY MUD!

OUCH! OK, RASHER — NO NEED TO BE SO TOUCHY ABOUT IT! I'LL CHOOSE OTHER WEAPONS!

SKID

SCRAPE!

AND I CHOOSE WATER PISTOLS!

ZOOM!

EVERSO OH! IN THAT CASE I'LL BE BACK IN A SEC!

THEN— MUMSY SAYS I MUSTN'T GET WET IN CASE I CATCH A COLDY-WOLDY.

EH?

THIS IS HOPELESS! YOU CAN CHOOSE THE WEAPONS!

SWOOSH!

SWOOSH!

GOODY! I KNOW JUST WHAT TO CHOOSE...

CLAP! CLAP!

SWORDS? CONKERS? BOXING GLOVES?

...MUMSY'S NICE SCENT— I CHOOSE SCENTS AS MY WEAPONS!

SQUIRT

TOPPLE

AAGH! WHAT HAVE I DONE?

BACK HOME—

ALL IS NOT LOST! WITH THE HELP OF SOME GARLIC AND RAW ONION...

GARLIC CLOVES

ONION RINGS

... I CAN STILL BEAT THE SOFTY.

WAFT!

BUCKLE

SNIGGER! MY **SCENT'S** KNOCKED ALL THE **SENSE** FROM WALTER!

FOUL BREATH!

AIR PURIFIER

GASP! WHEEZE!

MARCH

PARACHUTE JUMPING

ERK!

WALTER, HIDING

OPEN STRETCH

THAT'S WHY I FIXED DADDY'S BRACES ACROSS THE HALL!

NOW, GO AWAY, YOU NASTY BOY!

OOW! OOW!

PYDOING

BUMP!

SCRAPE

I'M NOT GOING TO BE SORRY — BUT THAT SOFTY IS...

FAN

SMOULDER

...I'M GOING TO TUNNEL MY WAY IN!

THAT CAN'T BE MY TUMMY— IT'S NOT NEARLY DINNER-TIME!

RUMBLE!

CRUMBS! I MUST HAVE HIT A WATER PIPE! GNASHER! HELP!

SWOOSH!

AT LEAST IT COOLED MY TROUSERS DOWN!

TURN

BUMP!

LET THAT BE A LESSON TO YOU, NAUGHTY MENACE!

NO MORE MISTER NICE GUY!

I'M GOING TO FIND OUT HOW WALTER'S GOING TO MAKE ME SORRY.

In Walter's bedroom—

ARGH! NOW I KNOW— WALTER'S...

... GOT MEASLES— AND SO DO I NOW!

TOLD YOU YOU'D BE SORRY! NA-NA-NA-NANA!

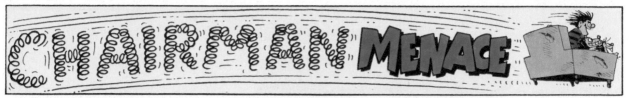

GNASHER AND GNIPPER

BALLET BULLY

WALTER'S NOT RUSHING TO SCHOOL AS USUAL! I DON'T BELIEVE IT!

← READER'S VOICE

TO SCHOOL

IT'S P.E. TODAY— I HATE GYM!

SCRAPE!

ALMOST WALKING BACKWARDS →

YAHOO! P.E. TODAY. WONDER IF IT'LL BE WEIGHT-LIFTING, OR BOXING, OR...

BUMP!

AND THAT'S WHY I HATE IT — IT'S FRIGHTFULLY ROUGH!

But—
SORRY, BOYS, I'VE HURT MY FOOT—THE GIRLS' P.E. TEACHER WILL TAKE YOUR CLASS TODAY.

EH?

P E

WE'RE GOING TO HAVE A DANCE CLASS TODAY, BOYS!

P E

GOODY-GOODY!

CLAP!

BUMP!

SWOON

SKIP

PRANCE

CLUMP!

BUMP!

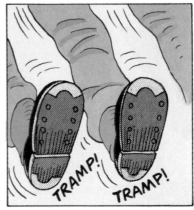

I ALSO LOVED...

...BLOWING BUBBLES!

SQUEEZE

SQUEEZE

BABIES' GAMES WERE FUN AS WELL!

GRAB

RING-A-RING-A-ROSIES! A POCKET-FULL OF POSIES! ATISHOO! ATISHOO!...

LET GO! UNHAND ME!

WHIRL

...OK~ALL FALL DOWN!

OOMFF!

THUMP!

ZOOM!

SNIVEL! IT WAS YOUR NAUGHTY SON!

TIME TO RUN AWAY!

HAVEN'T PLAYED WITH ONE OF THESE SINCE I WAS A LAD!

TWIRL

COME TO DADDY, LADDY! AS YOU'RE SO FOND OF BABIES' GAMES AND TOYS...

TUG

SCRAPE

...YOU'LL BE TREATED LIKE A BABY TILL YOU LEARN TO ACT YOUR AGE!

SIMPER! HOW CUTE! HE **IS** ACTING HIS AGE! HE'S HAVING A TANTRUM!

CAN'T LOOK!

BABY

MENACE MEETINGS and GREETINGS

CASTLE CASTAWAYS

HOME AT LAST AFTER A HARD DAY'S...

...WAH!

SPLUNGE!

WH-WHAT'S ALL THIS?

THIS IS CASTLE MENACE AND YOUR ATTACK HAS BEEN BEATEN!

ENOUGH OF THIS NONSENSE— LET ME IN!

IF YOU INSIST!..

TUG

THAT'S NOT A GOOD IDEA!

ARGH! PULL IT UP! PULL IT UP!

THUD!

SQUASH!

TOLD YOU IT WASN'T!

HUSH, DEAR! I CAN—PUFF— SEE I'M GOING TO HAVE TO USE MY SUPERIOR BRAIN POWER HERE!

TUG

BLOW

ACHE

LET ME...

THROB

...SO I'LL BATTER MY WAY IN! I KNOW ALL ABOUT GETTING INTO CASTLES, DEAR!

BUT...

IN OLD CASTLES, THEY WOULD USE BOILING OIL— BUT I CAN MAKE DO WITH DAD'S GREASE GUN!

PRESS

SQUIRT!

HEH-HEH!

I'VE HAD ENOUGH OF THIS NONSENSE TOO— I'LL CAPTURE CASTLE MENACE!

SLIP

WE SURRENDER!

HOW DID YOU MANAGE IT?

EASY! I THREATENED TO CUT OFF HIS SUPPLIES...

TO STARVE HIM OUT! JUST GOING TO DO THAT! CAN'T TEACH ME ABOUT CASTLES!

NO, BUT I CAN TEACH YOU HOW TO DEAL WITH DENNIS!

SMUG

...IT WAS HIS "BEANO" SUPPLY I THREATENED TO CUT OFF!

EVEN A REAL CASTLE WOULDN'T STAND A CHANCE AGAINST MY MUM!

TUG

DOME, SWEET DOME

HADRIAN THE MENACE!

BAA!

BAA!

LOTTUS PAINUS!

USSES SOREUS!

CRUNCH!

DENNIS THE CONQUEROR!

I SAY! LIQUIDISED SNAILS, GARLIC AND FROG'S LEGS! WHIMPER!

SPLASH!

SWOOSH!

WHIRR

ALFRED THE GREAT MENACE!

MUST'VE BEEN THE CURRIED CABBAGE I FED HIM!

SHRIEK! RASHER'S BURPS HAVE BURNT MY ANGEL CAKES!

WAFTY BURPS!

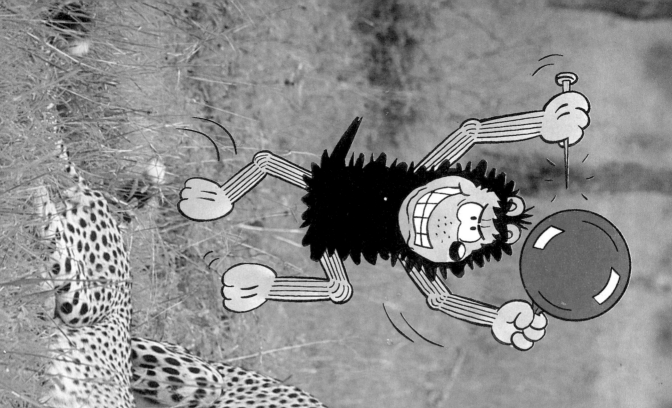

QUIET AROUND HERE!

GNASHER'S SURPRISE!

HEH-HEH! I'D BETTER FOLLOW HIM!

ZZZZ!

READ ALL ABOUT IT — GNASHER'S SLEEPWALKING!

WHISPER →

SSSH! BE QUIET — OR ELSE!

ZZZZ!

COTTON WOOL →

SSSH! BE QUIET — OR ELSE!

NNNN

COTTON WOOL

SSSH! BE QUIET — OR ELSE!

OH, NO!

ARMY CAMP

SSSH! BE QUIET — OR ELSE!

ZZZZ!

POP

POP

POP

ARMY CAMP

ZZZZ!

HMM! WHY IS IT SO DANGEROUS TO WAKE A SLEEPWALKER ANYWAY?

SCRATCH

I'LL FIND OUT! COME ON, GNASHER! WAKEN UP!

SHAKE

SHAKE

SHAKE

GEH? SNORT!

DOH!

THUMP!

GNASHEE! GNASHEE!

OOOH! I'VE FOUND OUT WHY IT'S DANGEROUS BECAUSE THE FIRST THING A SLEEPER DOES WHEN HE'S WAKENED IS THUMP HIS ALARM CLOCK! GROAN!

 KNOCK! KNOCK! **MENACE THERE?**

KNOCK!
KNOCK!

KNOCKING ON DOORS AND RUNNING AWAY CAN BE GREAT FUN—I DON'T HAVE TO RUN THIS TIME, THOUGH...

... WALTER'S TOO SCARED TO SEE WHO IS AT THE DOOR!

WH-WHO COULD THAT B-BE?

GNASHEE!

KNOCK ON THIS DOOR AND YOU'VE GOT TO RUN REALLY FAST!

WHAP!
WHAP!

GNESH!

GURRRRR!

POLICE STATION

IT'S THE POLICE STATION!

ZOOM!

TRIAL and TERROR

I'M NOT JUMPING O-OVER THAT! I'M TOO HIGH OFF THE GROUND ALREADY! SNIVEL!

BEANOTOWN HORSE TRIALS

WHAT A WIMP—LET'S SHOW HIM HOW IT'S DONE, RASHER!

RUMBLE

NOT QUITE WHAT I HAD IN MIND!

CLAMBER

STILL, WALTER SHOULD BE ABLE TO JUMP IT NOW!

CRACK! CRACK!

THUD!

IT'S THE WATER-JUMP NEXT!

WATER JUMP?

JUST WHAT I NEED AFTER ALL THAT CLIMBING!

VAROOOM!

EEK! RASHER'S TROTTERS HAVE STOPPED TROTTING AND STARTED GALLOPING!

HOI! YOU'RE MEANT TO JUMP THE WATER JUMP—NOT DRINK IT!

SUCK

WAH!

SPLUTCH!

A MUD JUMP'S MORE FUN ANYWAY! SNIGGER! RASHER DRANK ALL THE WATER!

SOON—

THIS'LL MAKE SURE RASHER GETS OVER...

THROW

...ER—THROUGH THIS JUMP!

CRASH!

OH, I SAY! BAD SHOW!

CHEW! CHOMP!

BEANOTOWN HORSE TRIALS

POLICE

IN COURT—

GROAN! WE'RE HAVING REAL HORSE TRIALS NOW!

THIS RIDER AND HIS HORSE—ER—PIG ARE GUILTY!

THUD!

HEH-HEH! THAT'S WHAT THEY GET FOR BREAKING MY JUMPS!

ON YER BIKE!

DAD'S AFTER ME FOR PUTTING SALT IN THE SUGAR BOWL— SO I'M HIDING IN HERE!

ZOOM!

EH?

HE'S IN THERE!

I KNOW YOU'RE IN THERE— YOU'RE SURROUNDED, DENNIS!

MY BIKE— MY GETAWAY!

JUST COMING, DAD!

TSK! MAYBE I SHOULD HAVE OPENED THE DOOR BEFORE I CAME OUT! SNIGGER!

GNASHEE!

GLOOPSH!

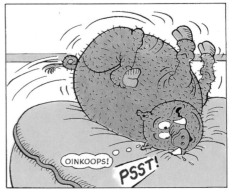

SOFTY? HARDLY!

DENNIS AND WALTER
CLUB TOGETHER

YOU SHOULD JOIN MENSA, MY LOVELY ONE. IT'S FOR CLEVER CHAPPIES LIKE YOU.

I AM, AM I NOT, MUMSIE?

$E = MC^2$

MENSA CLUB ROOMS

OPEN

EGG HEADS

LOOK! SMARTY-PANTS, JUST LIKE YOU, WALTER.

WE'LL SEE!

MENSA CLUB ROOMS

OPEN

So --

WANT TO JOIN MENACEA? THE CLUB FOR MENACES!

LIKE US!

I'D TAKE GNASHER FOR A WALK IN THE PARK, STOPPING TO SMELL THE ROSES!

SWEET SMELLING PONG!

GNO! GNO!

NO!

A MENACE WOULD LET MONTY GO FOR A JOG!

OH, NO!

I SAY!

EEK!

TEA ROOM

WAAAH!

MAD MOUSE!

DASH!

THUD!

SNEEZY DOES IT!

Different Class

A LOT OF DOG-WASH!

FOR ONCE ALL IS QUIET IN THE MENACE HOUSEHOLD...

WHAT'S THAT..?

HUM-M-M!

SNIFF! SNIFF!

GHASTLY NIFF

FAINT

SWOON

YOU'VE BEEN ROLLING ABOUT IN RASHER'S PIG-STY AGAIN, HAVEN'T YOU, GNASHER?

PUNGENT PONG

SMELL

WILT

FAT-FREE BACON!

EVERY DOG HAS ITS DAY

A KNOCKOUT PARTY!

WHAT ARE YOU DOING, WIMPISH WALTER?

I'M HAVING A GARDEN PICNIC PARTY FOR MY FRIENDS...

BALLOONS

A SUDDEN ATTACK OF BRAVADO—

... AND YOU'RE NOT MY FRIEND— SO THERE!

I'M GLAD OF THAT— I WOULDN'T COME TO YOUR PARTY IF YOU PAID ME!

RASP!

MY DENNIS IS GOING TO HAVE A GARDEN PICNIC PARTY JUST LIKE WALTER'S— ISN'T THAT SWEET?

POP

HELLO, FRIENDS.

WINK

WELCOME, FELLOW MENACES!

GRRRR!

GNASH!

POP

I'M GOING TO TRAIN YOU AS GUARD DOGS— THEN YOU CAN GUARD THE HOUSE!

SNORE!

Z-z-z

HERE COMES SOFTY WALTER— SCARE HIM OFF!

SNURFLE! Z-Z-Z!

OOOOH, IT LOOKED AT ME—THE NASTY DOGGY LOOKED AT ME!

THAT WASN'T MUCH OF A TEST—WE NEED SOMEONE TOUGHER!

FAINT

THERE—SCARE MUM OFF!

GNIP! GNIP!

CAN'T HAVE YOU DIRTYING MY CLEAN PATH!

GNERK!

MUM'S NOT SCARED OF MUCH!

SWEEP SWEEP

LATER— CURLY'S GOING TO HELP TRAIN YOU, DOGS— LOOK FIERCE AND SCARE HIM OFF!

H'MM! I'VE GOT A RAGGEDY NAIL!

HOPELESS! I'LL SHOW YOU HOW!

G-R-O-W-L!

ST-STEADY ON, DENNIS!

I CAN DO THAT!

SHRIEK!!

WE'RE ALL HAVING T-TO WORK FOR OUR GRUB N-NOW...

ZOOM!

ZOOM!

COME BACK! WAH!

ZOOM!

...GNASHER SCARED OFF THE LAD WHO WAS DELIVERING OUR GROCERIES!

BEAGINNINGS